MONUMENTS

MASTERPIECES OF ARCHITECTURE

LAURA BROOKS

SMITHMARK

This edition published in 1996 by SMITHMARK Publishers,
a division of U.S. Media Holdings, Inc., 16 East 32nd Street, New York, NY 10016.

SMITHMARK books are available for bulk purchase for sales promotion and premium use.
For details write or call the manager of special sales,
SMITHMARK Publishers, 16 East 32nd Street, New York, NY 10016; (212) 532-6600.

This book was designed and produced by Todtri Productions Limited
P.O. Box 572, New York, NY 10116-0572 FAX: (212) 279-1241

Printed and bound in Singapore

Library of Congress Catalog Card Number 97-066042
ISBN 0-7651-9199-7

Author: Laura Brooks

Publisher: Robert M. Tod
Editorial Director: Elizabeth Loonan
Book Designer: Mark Weinberg
Senior Editor: Cynthia Sternau
Project Editor: Ann Kirby
Photo Editor: Edward Douglas
Picture Researchers: Meiers Tambeau, Laura Wyss
Production Coordinator: Jay Weiser
Typesetting: Command-O Design

CONTENTS

INTRODUCTION

In the fifth century B.C., the Greek historian Herodotus described seven "wonders" known the world over for their size, material, engineering, beauty, and symbolic power. Scattered across the countries adjoining the Mediterranean Sea, these so-called Seven Wonders of the Ancient World included the Great Pyramid of Chephren at Giza, the Hanging Gardens of Babylon, the Statue of Zeus at Olympia, the Temple of Artemis at Ephesus, the Mausoleum at Halicarnassus, the Colossus of Rhodes, and the Pharos (lighthouse) of Alexandria. These "wonders" were among the world's first recognized monuments.

From the beginning of recorded history to the present day, people have erected monuments. In about 7000 B.C., a city wall was erected at Jericho, in one of the world's earliest civilized societies. Since that time, people in every corner of the earth have constructed not only walls but temples, statues, towers, markers, tombs, and other structures that define our public spaces, extol our ideals, characterize our societies, and symbolize who we are. A monument expresses the collective goals, joys, and sorrows of a society.

The word "monument" comes from the Latin word *moneo*, which means to remind. The Romans used the word to describe their public statues and buildings, and this intriguing ancient definition points to the heart of what a monument is. A monument is anything that *reminds* us of a person, an event, or an idea from our collective past. A monument is a way in which society remembers its past and formulates its present identity. People have always intended monuments to be permanent; they are meant to last forever in order to educate and remind future generations of values the society deems significant. Therefore, monuments are almost always made of lasting materials—stone, marble, bronze, steel, or iron.

However, constructing monuments in permanent materials does not always ensure their survival in the face of natural disasters, war, and dramatic changes in society's standards. Of the remarkable Seven Wonders of the Ancient World, only one survives today—the Great Pyramid in Giza, Egypt. The seemingly indestructible Colossus of Rhodes stood only fifty-six years after its completion in 282 B.C., at which point the gigantic marble and bronze statue was felled by an earthquake and remained prostrate on the ground for nearly a millennium until it was finally disassembled and carried away in the seventh century A.D. On the opposite end of

RIGHT: A foreboding colossal statue of the ancient Egyptian pharaoh Ramses II guards the entrance to the Temple of Abu Simbel in Egypt, built thirty-five hundred years ago.

the spectrum, some monuments that were originally meant to be temporary survive today because they gain status over the years. The Eiffel Tower in Paris, France, for example, was erected for the 1889 International Exposition, and shortly thereafter was slated for destruction. However, over the years the tower became synonymous with the city of Paris, and so remains a permanent structure in the physical and emotional landscape of France.

In addition to permanence, the word "monument" also connotes something public, or at least visible to the public if not fully accessible. Even monuments that have private or semi-private spaces, such as a royal palace or the papal residence, have a public aspect—a façade or an architectural element that proclaims importance and a message to the public outside.

Monuments are often symbolic. The thirty-six Doric columns of the Lincoln Memorial in Washington, D.C., symbolize the number of states in the Union at the time of the President's death. In the Statue of Liberty in New York City, Liberty is personified as a robed woman standing on broken chains, which represent tyranny.

But these definitions of monuments—public, permanent, historically important, symbolic—can apply to a surprising range of things. A glance at the dictionary definition of "monument" yields various meanings, including a building, a sculpture, an inscribed marker, anything venerated for its historic significance and enduring achievement, a tradition, an object used as a marker, or any written document. The list of sites managed by the United States National Park Service includes a stunning variety of things referred to as "monuments," including natural sites like Death Valley in California and Nevada (considered by the government to be the largest national monument in the country), battlefields such as Little Bighorn in Montana, and perennial favorites like the Statue of Liberty and the Jefferson Memorial. In this regard, the modern world is not much different from the ancient one—the Seven Wonders of the Ancient World included everything from a statue to a garden and a lighthouse.

How does society remember its past? What factors affect its collective memory? From Easter Island to New York City, monuments commemorate heroes, celebrate cultural icons, function in innumerable religions, and define identity. Although monuments are as varied as the people that create them, the creation of monuments is nothing less than quintessentially human.

RIGHT: The original function of the mysterious colossal stone figures on Easter Island remains unknown, as well as how these heavy stones were moved and sculpted, and by whom.

LEFT: The Eiffel Tower in Paris was a highly controversial monument when it was constructed for the International Exposition of 1889, but today it stands as a symbol of France.

RIGHT: Callanish Stone Circle, Western Isles. Mysterious ancient stone circles such as this appear across the British Isles. Their original function is unclear, but they were probably used as sites of ritual for prehistoric cultures.

CHAPTER ONE

LANDMARKS OF TIME'S PASSING

LEFT: Shown here is one of four enormous faces of what many think of as Big Ben. The name was actually first applied to the clock's sonorous bell, installed in 1856 by Sir Benjamin Hall.

Monuments function as historical documents. In fact, "reading" a monument is similar to reading a book. As with a novel, certain elements of a monument—including scale, setting, and the gestures and expressions of human figures—convey meaning. Monuments can narrate a tale or evoke a significant historical event. But monuments do more than tell a story about history. As visual objects, they elicit responses of nostalgia, pride, empathy, sorrow, compassion, and respect more powerfully than the written word. Monuments cause people to feel connected to a collective past, a common tradition, and a shared experience.

Monuments of Civic Pride

Some monuments are synonymous with the cities they occupy. The Eiffel Tower *is* Paris; the Colosseum *is* Rome. For the residents of the world's greatest cities, public monuments define their civic identity. Town governments often reproduce their monuments on banners, city seals, and other official objects. In some cases, inhabitants deliberately construct monuments that express their city's ideals, status, or character. In other cases, the association of a monument with a city is unintentional, and only develops over a period of years or even centuries.

In medieval and Renaissance Italy, bell towers were commonly erected as symbols of a city's wealth and prominence. The *campanile* at once dominated the surrounding landscape and defined the silhouette of the town's cityscape. When its construction began in 1174, the Leaning Tower of Pisa was intended to be just such a prestigious symbol. The tower was erected as part of the cathedral complex of the city-state of Pisa in central Italy. However, the ill-fated monument began to list to one side

RIGHT: At the Colosseum, the ancient Romans enjoyed gladiatorial combat, horse races, naval demonstrations, and other, more gruesome spectacles. Even in its ruined state, the Colosseum remains an impressive monument.

LEFT: In Pisa, Italy, the famous Leaning Tower lists precariously to one side. Its weak foundations caused it to lean even before its completion in the twelfth century.

even before its completion, and all subsequent efforts to stabilize its weak foundations have failed. Today, the Leaning Tower of Pisa is the most famous of the Tuscan bell towers precisely because of its curious angle.

Another famous bell tower, Big Ben, is dear to the hearts of Londoners and a symbol of that English city. Its name refers not to the tower itself but to its largest bell, which was cast by Sir Benjamin Hall and tips the scales at 13.5 tons. Big Ben was constructed between 1858 and 1859 in a Gothic Revival style that visually unites it with the adjacent Houses of Parliament. A light atop the tower is lit when the House of Commons is in session. The gargantuan clock tower measures more than 320

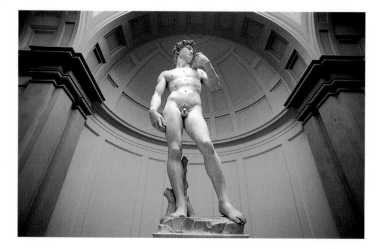

feet (98 meters) tall, with four clock dials 23 feet (7 meters) in diameter, and numerals 2 feet (.6 meter) high.

The most famous of city towers, perhaps, was not meant to tell time or to ring bells at all. In fact, the Eiffel Tower of Paris was not even meant to be permanent. Gustave Eiffel created the mammoth structure on the Left Bank of the Seine for the 1889 International Exposition as a display of the potential of new industrial metals in architecture. At that time, the tower was highly controversial. Many nineteenth-century Parisians criticized *la Tour Eiffel* as a hideous eyesore, and others feared it was simply unsafe. The Eiffel Tower was slated for destruction in 1909, but it survived because of its practical use as a radio tower. Today, hordes of tourists wait in line to take the elevator or to climb the tortuous stairs to the top and buy miniature replicas of the tower from the ubiquitous souvenir shops. The Eiffel Tower is now the most recognizable monument in Paris.

Though it is not a tower, Michelangelo's famous statue of David once served as a civic monument for the city of Florence. Michelangelo began sculpting the statue of the biblical figure in 1501 at the age of twenty-six. Originally, the sculpture was intended to be placed high above the ground, where it would have embellished one of the buttresses of the Florence cathedral, but it never made it to that location. The city fathers were so enchanted with the statue that they placed in the Palazzo Vecchio, the heart of Renaissance Florence. In the city square,

ABOVE: Michelangelo's statue of the biblical David was originally intended to be placed high above the ground on the Cathedral of Florence. The city fathers were so impressed with the sculpture, however, that they installed it in the main city square, where it stood as a symbol of civic pride. Today, the masterpiece is preserved in a Florence museum.

RIGHT: New York's Statue of Liberty holds her flame to the wind, a beacon for travelers arriving from afar. The statue, a gift to the United States from France, was dedicated in 1886 and became a national monument in 1924.

David became a metaphor for the proud, strong republic of Florence poised for battle against the larger city-states surrounding it. Now preserved in a museum and replaced with a copy on the intended site, the young, vital, muscular figure recalls the heroic figures of the ancient past and the powerful cities where they once lived.

Monuments and National Ideals

Many monuments embody the virtues a society holds dear—liberty, justice, prudence, and equality, for example. In the city squares of ancient Greece and Rome, sculptors erected stone statues representing time, beauty, and other allegorical themes or attributes in the form of humans or animals. Likewise, in nineteenth-century Europe and America, sculptures personifying civic virtues were displayed in prominent places, celebrating political and philosophical ideals.

The Statue of Liberty symbolizes the principles of the American political system and captures the spirit of freedom's role in United States history. The Statue of Liberty is surely the most famous colossal statue since the Colossus of Rhodes. The

ABOVE: The venerable clock tower that overlooks the Houses of Parliament in London is a symbol of England's capital city. It was constructed during the 1850s in the Neo-Gothic style.

Colossus was destroyed in the third century B.C., but the existence of the Statue of Liberty testifies to its lasting effect. Like its ancient predecessor, which overlooked the ocean from the port of Rhodes, the Statue of Liberty graces the entrance to New York's harbor with an imposing grandeur. The monument, designed by the French sculptor Frédéric Bartholdi, was dedicated in 1886 and became a national monument in 1924. The woman with the flowing robes, spiked crown, and flaming torch was originally called *Liberty Enlightening the World*. In her left hand, Liberty holds a book inscribed with the date of July 4, 1776, recalling the American Revolution. Large shackles symbolizing tyranny lie broken at her feet. The French government gave the monument to the United States in commemoration of American independence, and today the 150-foot (46-meter) statue is a symbol of the American ideals of liberty and freedom.

The Monument to the Third International is another }ambitious symbol of national idealism, but, unlike the Statue of Liberty, it was, unfortunately, never realized. The Soviet architect Vladimir Evgrafovic Tatlin (1885–1953) planned the monument in between 1919 and 1920 to house the legislative offices of the new revolutionary government in Leningrad. Tatlin conceived of a gigantic spiral of wood, iron, and glass that would reach the almost inconceivable height of 1,300 feet (396 meters). It was to span the Neva River, and encompass three glass-walled buildings that would revolve at different speeds—one would take a day to complete a turn, one a month, and one a year—while light beams projected skyward from the roof. The Monument to the Third International presented a vision of the technological utopia and reshaping of society that Communism promised. Its unprecedented form suggested a break from history and a new architectural and social order. Had it been achieved, it would have combined the elements of time, movement, energy, and scale in a way never before realized in one monument.

Reverent Spaces

Religious monuments of all faiths, past and present, share a sense of awe and quiet grandeur. Whether a church, a mosque, a temple, or an ancient pyramid, these spaces cause visitors to slow their pace and drop their voices to a whisper. Religious monuments are usually very large in scale and convey a feeling of reverence, beauty, contemplation, and spirituality found in no other type of monument.

The site on which many religious monuments stand is often more important than the monument itself. The Pyramid of the Sun at Teotihuacán, Mexico, for example, was erected above a cave that was believed to be the entrance to the underworld. Only priests had access to its inner sanctum, and the pyramid was the site not only of religious ceremonies but also of human sacrifice. The pyramid is oriented toward the rising sun, reflecting the Aztez belief that astronomy was of paramount importance. The ancient Mexicans carefully observed the heavens for signs and omens that affected their everyday lives. In fact, nearly 88 percent of the buildings of pre-Columbian Mexico face the

RIGHT: The Wailing Wall in Jerusalem is all that remains of the biblical Temple of Solomon, destroyed by the ancient Romans in A.D. 70. Ever since, the site has drawn crowds of the faithful, many of whom press small slips of paper containing prayers into the cracks of this venerable wall.

The enormous Pyramid of the Sun in Teotihuacán, Mexico, is just one of several pyramids that once lined an avenue of this ancient Meso-American city. The ancient Aztecs believed that the pyramid sat at the entrance to the underworld.

east. The stepped pyramids of Mexico, constructed with a system of inner piers, exterior steps, and rubble faced with smooth masonry, differ from the pyramids of ancient Egypt, which were erected with solid blocks of stone. Teotihuacán was the largest and most impressive city of the Aztecs, counting 200,000 inhabitants in its heyday around A.D. 600. The Pyramid of the Sun, the largest pyramid in the western hemisphere, was just one of many temples lining one of the central avenues of the city.

Like the Pyramid of the Sun, the Wailing Wall in Jerusalem stands on a hallowed site. The Wailing Wall is the last vestige of the great ancient Jewish temple once located in Jerusalem. In A.D.70 , the Roman emperor Titus broke through the wall and burned and pillaged the temple. For the Romans, the event was a military coup. Back home in Rome, the Romans depicted the spoils of the temple being paraded triumphantly through the streets on the carved reliefs on the Arch of Titus. For the Jews,

however, the destruction of the temple was one of the greatest tragedies of their history. Today, the Wailing Wall is their most holy site. The 50-foot (15-meter) Wailing Wall, which is probably one of the ancient retaining walls of the temple, is situated on the western side of Temple Mount. The faithful stand before it to lament the loss of the temple and to draw close to the Holy of Holies, an inner room of the temple now occupied by a mosque. The tradition of praying at the Wall began between A.D. 200 and 300 , and the monument came to be called the Wailing Wall due to the many tears shed before it as a symbol of loss,

LEFT: The catacombs of Rome contain the remains of the city's early citizens. For early Christians, the catacombs were a place of worship as well as a place of burial. Elsewhere in Rome, at the Capuchin Cemetery, shown here, the skeletons themselves constitute decorative elements.

struggle, hope, and freedom. The tiny pieces of paper pressed into the cracks of the Wailing Wall's great stones contain the prayers of the faithful; they bear witness to the power of this monument.

Not unlike the Wailing Wall, the Kaaba of Mecca also holds a fundamental place in the history of religion. Mecca is the center of the Islamic faith, and Muslims from every corner of the globe endeavor to make a pilgrimage (called the *hajj*) at least once in their lifetimes to its location in the desert of Saudi Arabia. Mecca is the birthplace of the religion's founder, Muhammad, who is believed to have meditated in the desert wilderness

before receiving the call to deliver a spiritual message to his people. At the center of the crowded courtyard at the Great Mosque of Mecca stands a curious black cube-shaped building called the Kaaba that is the spiritual and physical epicenter of Islam. The origins of the ancient Kaaba are shrouded in mystery, but tradition has it that the angel Gabriel gave to Abraham a black stone that is housed in the Kaaba. Today, the Kaaba serves as an integral part of the pilgrimage ritual.

For the early Christians, the locations of their first sanctuaries were also symbolically charged. The catacombs, subterranean cemeteries that lie underneath the streets of Rome, mark

LEFT: This illustration reconstructs the full splendor of the ancient Athenian Parthenon as it once stood on the Acropolis during the heyday of Greek civilization in the fifth century B.C.

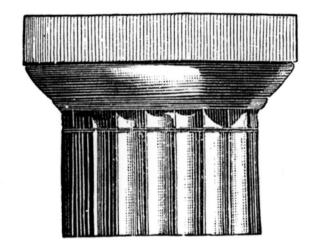

the burial places of early Christian martyrs. The catacombs form a sprawling network of labyrinthine tunnels that cover hundreds of miles beneath the legendary city. More than sixty extensive catacombs house tens of thousands of tombs containing the remains of Christians who wanted to be buried near revered martyrs of the first through the fourth centuries A.D. The Roman emperors forbade Christian worship until A.D.313, so the catacombs were secret places of worship as well as underground cemeteries for the early Christians. Even after Christianity was officially recognized, the catacombs continued to be used until the eighth or ninth centuries, when they were finally abandoned. They remained undisturbed until their rediscovery in the sixteenth and seventeenth centuries. The catacombs are composed of lengthy, narrow passages flanked by superimposed rows of rectangular, human-sized niches cut into the earth. The early Christians wrapped their dead in white shrouds, and often sealed the tombs with marble slabs. At certain intervals, rooms were carved out of the earth to serve as chapels or family tombs. These spaces were decorated with exquisite fresco paintings representing religious themes. Many of the paintings are remarkably well preserved, and provide some of the best examples of early Christian art.

The location of the Parthenon in Athens was strategic as well as symbolic. Situated high above the ancient city on the Acropolis, a massive limestone outcrop that was once fortified, the Parthenon is a relic from the ancient past. This majestic monument was constructed between 448 and 432 B.C., when Athens was at the height of her power, by the architects Ictinus and Callicrates. The Age of Pericles, named after the ruler who commissioned the monument, was an unparalleled time of Athenian prosperity. The Parthenon is the crowning achievement of this era, and is synonymous with the mature classical phase of Greek art. With its four perfectly proportioned façades of Doric columns, the Parthenon represents the embodiment of the Greek architectural principles of harmony and order. The mighty temple was dedicated to the goddess Athena, patron of the city and one of the supreme goddesses of antiquity. It housed a colossal statue of Athena that was richly decorated with gold, fabrics, and other precious materials. The temple was subsequently used as a Byzantine church dedicated to the Virgin, then as a Catholic cathedral, and later as a mosque. Today it is a landmark of the classical aesthetic and a credit to the ingenuity of the ancient Greeks.

LEFT: Here are excellent examples of the three orders of classical architecture (shown top to bottom): a Doric capital, an Ionic capital from the Erechtheum of the Acropolis, and a Corinthian capital.

RIGHT: Ancient Greek female figures in the form of columns gaze out over the city of Athens from the Acropolis. These elegant statues express the classical ideals of order, symmetry, beauty, and grace.

BELOW: The Parthenon, which stands on the Acropolis overlooking the city of Athens, is the quintessential monument of ancient Greece. The Parthenon was built between 448 and 432 B.C., when the Athenians enjoyed a period of economic, political, and cultural prosperity.

LEFT: Inside the Parthenon was a colossal statue of the goddess Athena, the patron deity of Athens. The *Athena Parthenos*, a gold and ivory work sculpted by Phidias, was dedicated c. 438 B.C. and destroyed during antiquity.

ZUM ANDENKEN
AN DIE EINMUETH.SE
SIEGREICHE ERHEBUNG
DES DEUTSCHEN VOLKES
UND AN DIE
WIEDERAUFRICHTUNG
DES DEUTSCHEN REICHES
1870—1871.

ABOVE: In the nineteenth century, sculptors constructed numerous symbolic monuments in Europe's capitals that recalled the monuments of the glorious classical past. This one, a personification of *Germania*, graces a square in Rudesheim, Germany, and celebrates the unification of the German states into a single nation in 1870–71.

RIGHT: An exterior view of the magnificent Dome of the Rock (c. A.D. 691) in Jerusalem, a holy site for Moslems, Christians, and Jews.

Monuments of Mystery

Some of the world's most famous monuments are those about which almost nothing is known. In fact, the mystery surrounding these monuments propels our fascination with them and heightens the sense of intrigue they carry. In many cases, these monuments are vestiges of ancient civilizations the modern world no longer understands.

On a now-desolate landscape on Easter Island in the South Pacific, endless rows of colossal stone figures bear witness to a lost culture. Sometimes referred to as Moai statues, each one of these enormous stone images is carved from soft volcanic lava and stands higher than 30 feet (9 meters). They sit on raised platforms, the shape of the human body only vaguely suggested. Each figure is topped with a "head," the back of which is missing. The now-empty eye sockets were originally filled with colored shells, which must have given the effigies an even more frightening aspect. No one knows how each 16-ton stone was moved or erected. These mask-like images may represent ancestral figures, but European explorers in the seventeenth century remarked that the local people had long forgotten the purpose of these giants and even had pushed some of them into the sea. Their meaning has been lost with the passing of time, and the significance of these imposing, compelling images remains unexplained.

We are better informed about Stonehenge, a monument consisting of giant stones or megaliths erected about four thousand years ago. Stonehenge is a *cromlech*, or ritual circle, of which there are numerous examples in Britain. The large stones, some of which have fallen or disintegrated, form a circle surrounded by a ditch. How did the ancients transport these gigantic sandstones and bluestones, the quarries for which have been located as far as 130 miles (209 kilometers) away from the site? The answer to this question remains a mystery. The entire structure is oriented toward the spot where the sun rises on the summer solstice, and it is likely that Stonehenge was the site of rituals centering on the sun.

LEFT: Ancient peoples moved gigantic stones over 100 miles (1.609 kilometers) to erect this cromlech, or ritual circle, at Stonehenge. The ring of stones is arranged to correspond with the rising of the sun at Summer Solstice.

BELOW: On Easter Island, faces of compelling stone statues gaze out from the past. Some believe these icons originally may have represented ancestral spirits watching over the living.

The Sphinx, erected in 2500 B.C., about five hundred years earlier than Stonehenge, stands majestically alongside the Great Pyramids of Giza in Egypt. The Sphinx is the oldest colossal sculpture to survive from the ancient world, and evokes the magnificence of these ancient masterpieces. The giant hybrid beast, with the body of a lion and the face of a man, forms part of the royal burial complex, where it was constructed alongside the pyramid of the pharaoh Chephren. In fact, the Sphinx bears what are believed to be the facial features and headdress of Chephren, while the body is in the form of a crouching lion. Though damaged in subsequent centuries, the Sphinx remains a potent monument to ancient royal power.

RIGHT: The Great Sphinx in Giza, Egypt, stands alongside the pyramids of the ancient pharaohs. The hybrid, mythical creature is thought to bear the facial features of the pharaoh Chephren, though erosion and vandalism in subsequent centuries have nearly obliterated the nose and mouth.

Technological Feats

Some monuments achieve their status because they represent a new or technically advanced idea. The use of non-traditional materials or a reinterpretation of traditional forms might mark the monument as important. Building on a larger scale than usual, or utilizing an innovative design also assures monumental notoriety.

The Opera House in Sydney, Australia, uses an ingenious design that highlights Sydney Harbor as the focal point of the

LEFT: The Place de la République in Paris is one of many squares in that city boasting a monumental symbolic statue erected toward the end of the nineteenth century. Here, a personification of Victory holds her laurel wreath on high.

LEFT: The Sydney Opera House is a technical marvel that now serves as a cultural center for Australia. Its innovative roof design resembles the sailboats in the adjoining Sydney Harbor and makes for pleasing acoustical qualities.

ABOVE: Tower Bridge in London was built in the nineteenth century in a Gothic revival style. Its imposing towers support a pedestrian walkway high above the drawbridge below, which allows boats into the harbor.

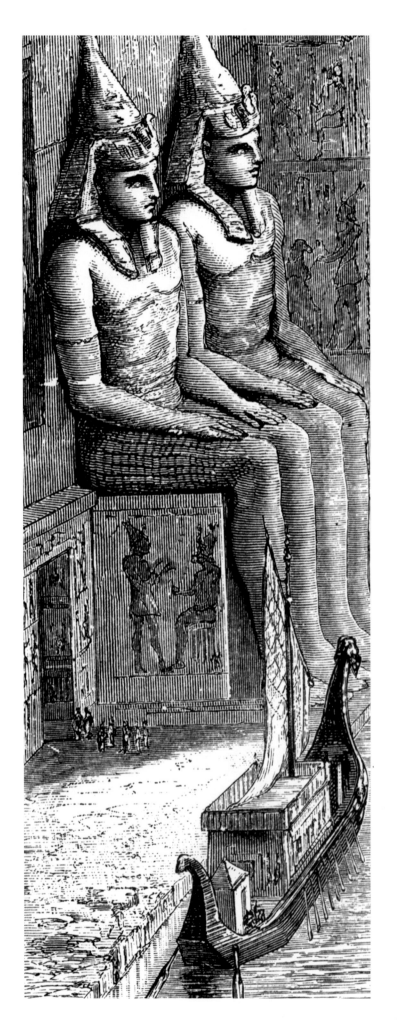

city. The Danish architect Jorn Utzon began the building in 1956 after winning a design competition, but it was not opened until 1973 due to construction delays. The roof design resembles sails inflated with air, and mirrors the sailboats anchored in the adjacent harbor. The design also alludes to the function of the building, since the shells bring to mind the acoustical resonance of a musical performance. The roof, often called Sails by the Sea, is a complex design made of more than two thousand sections held together with steel cable. The Opera House contains nearly one thousand rooms under its roof, including not only theaters and concert halls but also restaurants, bars, lounge areas, a library, offices, and dressing rooms.

For its day, London's Tower Bridge was a technical marvel. The bridge was built between 1886 and 1894 spanning the Thames River. Steam engines powered the drawbridge, which allowed oceangoing ships to enter the harbor of London. Pedestrians could walk along the upper deck of the bridge while ships were passing below. The bridge's square towers and Victorian style link it to the Tower of London, the medieval fortress that stands at its feet. The bridge is one of the city's most famous landmarks, affording panoramic views of London, its suburbs, and the Thames.

When the Egyptian pharaoh Ramses II commissioned the Temple of Abu Simbel 3500 years ago, he achieved a technical feat. The monumental tomb and temple were bored into the wall of a cliff, and four colossal seated statues of the pharaoh stood rigid and foreboding at its entrance. Even more technically impressive, however, was the moving of the temple in the twentieth century during the building of the Aswan Dam. The Aswan Dam, completed in 1964, dammed the Nile river about 600 miles (965 kilometers) south of Cairo in order to corral energy for the burgeoning population in the region. The newly created lake submerged many ancient Egyptian monuments and archeological sites, and threatened the Temple of Abu Simbel. Remarkably, workers cut the temple into two thousand pieces that together weighed nearly 40,000 tons, moved it 90 feet (27 meters) higher, and reassembled it safely out of the way of the rising flood waters.

Monuments in Metal

Toward the end of the nineteenth century, iron, steel, and other metals were utilized on a grand scale for the first time. The seemingly unlimited potential of this medium inspired architects and designers to stretch the limits of their material, offering new

LEFT: An early engraving of the ancient Temple of Abu Simbel shows an artist's rendition of an Egyptian galley passing through the famous site during a voyage along the Nile River.

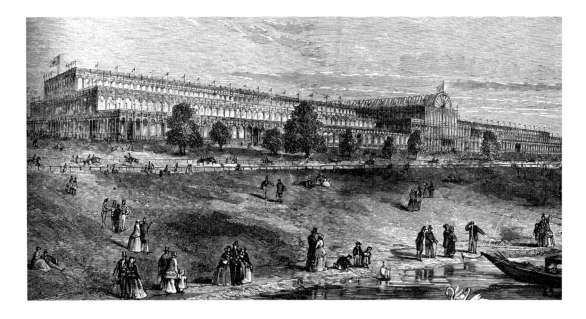

ABOVE: The Temple of Ramses II at Abu Simbel, Egypt, was saved from rising waters after the Aswan Dam was constructed in 1964. The temple was dismantled and reassembled 90 feet (27.5 meters) above its original location.

LEFT: A contemporary engraving shows the magnificent Crystal Palace, designed by Sir Joseph Paxon, and erected in London for the Great Exhibition of 1851. This unique monument was destroyed during the Second World War.

forms and innovative designs. By its very nature, metal lends itself to a skeletal appearance, and architects such as Joseph Paxton and Gustave Eiffel celebrated this aspect with monuments like the Crystal Palace and the Eiffel Tower. Metal remains an important material for modern monument builders.

In 1851, Sir Joseph Paxton designed the Crystal Palace in London in order to house the international exhibitions that were all the rage in Europe and America in the mid-nineteenth century. Paxton was not only an architect but also a greenhouse builder, and it is no surprise that the Crystal Palace was shaped like a giant greenhouse. But never before had a greenhouse been built on such a scale—the Crystal Palace was destined to accommodate the throngs of visitors that frequented international exhibitions. Its barrel-vaulted iron skeleton celebrated the

beauty of raw metal and glass, creating a weightless, airy quality well suited to an exhibition space. Sadly, the Crystal Palace was destroyed by fire in 1936.

Like the Crystal Palace, the Jefferson Westward Expansion Memorial in Saint Louis, better known as the Gateway Arch, celebrates the integrity of metal as a structure. The stainless-steel monument is a fusion of architecture and engineering, and commemorates the westward expansion of the United States between 1803 and 1890. Its architect, Eero Saarinen, presented the winning design in a competition in 1947, but the monument was not completed until 1966. The form is reminiscent of the triumphal arches of antiquity, but looks to the future with its seemingly elastic arc that can be seen from thirty miles away. At 630 feet high (192 meters), the Gateway Arch is America's tallest monument.

ABOVE: The Jefferson Westward Expansion Monument, also known as the Gateway Arch in St. Louis, Missouri, stands nearly 630 feet (192 meters) in height, and is America's tallest monument. Completed by the architect Eero Saarinen in 1964, the monument commemorates the westward expansion of the United States in the nineteenth century.

RIGHT: The ancient Egyptian Temple of Luxor was built in the reign of Amenhotep III as a temple to Amon. Ramses II and other pharaohs added their own monuments to the site, such as the colossal statues and the obelisk.

CHAPTER TWO

MONUMENTS TO POWER

Since the dawn of time, people in positions of power have constructed monuments to commemorate their accomplishments, celebrate their victories, and pay homage to their predecessors. In glorifying the reigns of the powerful, monuments influence public opinion and form an image of a society's rulers. It is not by chance that presidents, emperors, kings, queens, and other political leaders have erected more public monuments than any other type of individual or group in history.

Although political monuments are usually intended to be permanent, such monuments have often been demolished as a result of dramatic changes in the political climate. Some monuments were even destroyed not long after they had been erected. At the death of the Roman emperor Domitian (ruled A.D. 81–96), for example, nearly all of the public stone statues depicting the leader were dismantled and smashed to pieces. Throughout the empire, the image of the emperor, who was viewed as a ruthless warmonger and evildoer, was wiped from the collective memory of the society. The Romans referred to this practice as *damnatio memoriae*, which literally means to damn someone's memory. Centuries later, after the fall of communism in the former Soviet Union, a similar scene unfolded from the heart of Moscow to the squares of the provincial capitals. As the government crumbled, statues of Lenin and other Soviet leaders were summarily dismantled or destroyed.

Many political leaders look to ancient Rome as a model of political and military power. The Romans were also masters of the public political monument, and in subsequent centuries leaders have sought to emulate the ancient Romans and their monuments. From Napoleon to Thomas Jefferson, rulers have deliberately chosen classical forms for their public monuments. Monuments using classical columns, pristine marbles, an impressive scale, and other forms derived from the ancient world appear not only all over Europe but also in the cities and towns of America, Asia, and Africa—far beyond the outermost boundaries of the Roman empire and more distant than the Roman emperors ever dreamed.

LEFT: The Emperor Napoleon constructed the Arc de Triomphe in Paris using ancient Rome as his source of inspiration. The arch stands in the center of wide avenues that radiate out from the monument in a star pattern.

ABOVE: An early engraving recreates the bustling atmosphere of the Roman Forum in its heyday, showing an astonishingly wide variety of monuments to power and national sentiment.

The Triumphal Arch

The Romans erected triumphal arches throughout their territories in order to celebrate military victories. And with an empire that stretched west to the Iberian Peninsula, north to the British Isles, south to Africa, and east to modern-day Iran, they had plenty of victories to celebrate. Triumphal arches proclaiming the glory of Roman generals and their troops littered the squares of ancient Rome, and were a standard feature of Roman provincial capitals all over the empire. The triumphal arch has enjoyed a long life in the history of monuments, for its form has been borrowed and reinterpreted throughout the centuries.

The Arch of Titus in Rome celebrates the Roman army's capture of Jerusalem and the burning of the Temple in A.D. 70 Erected between the imperial fora and the Colosseum of Rome, the relief sculpture depicts a victorious Roman army bringing back the spoils of war. The Arch of Titus is a permanent example in stone of the many more temporary triumphal arches that

ABOVE: A detail from the Arch of Titus in Rome shows Jewish prisoners of war carrying spoils from the sack of the Temple in Jerusalem following the Roman victory in A.D. 70

were erected in Rome to welcome home victorious generals and their troops, as part of a ceremony that was like an ancient ticker-tape parade.

Seventeen hundred years later, in an unabashed borrowing of an ancient form, Napoleon Bonaparte emulated his ancient predecessors by erecting a triumphal arch in the heart of Paris. The Arc de Triomphe, built between 1833 and 1836, forms the epicenter of avenues that radiate outward from the monument in a star pattern. For Napoleon, who fashioned himself after the conquering Romans, the Arc de Triomphe symbolized his military victories abroad and stirred patriotism at home. Dramatic sculptures by François Rude embellish the sides, and the French Tomb of the Unknown Soldier lies below the giant arch.

French president François Mitterand's commissioning of the Grande Arche de la Défense in Paris proves that imitating the ancients did not stop with Napoleon. The great structure sits on the outskirts of Paris, at one end of an axis that aligns many of the city's most important sights, including the Louvre, the Champs-Elysées, and the Arc de Triomphe. The symbolically charged form, while modernized, forms a visual and historical link among great leaders in the history of France. When Mitterand took office in 1981, the president undertook a series of ambitious campaigns of monument building that included the new Paris Opera and the glass pyramids additions to the Louvre. With the Grande Arche in 1989, Mitterand's architects, Otto von Spreckelsen and Paul Andreu, greatly exceeded the scale of either the Arch of Titus or the Arc de Triomphe. The entire cathedral of Notre-Dame could stand under this truly monumental and modern triumphal arch.

LEFT: Dramatic relief sculptures on the side of the Arc de Triomphe in Paris depict the ideals of liberty and freedom. Like its ancient counterparts, the Arc de Triomphe is decorated with sculptures symbolizing the ideals of the nation at the time of its construction.

LEFT: The Grande Arche de la Défense outside of Paris is the post-modern answer to the historical triumphal arch. With a nod to the past, this towering structure looks to the future with a bold, minimalistic form and stark whiteness that characterize it as a product of the twentieth century.

RIGHT: The Arch of Constantine in Rome is just one of many triumphal arches erected by the ancient Roman emperors as a celebration of military victory. Decorated with relief sculptures depicting emperors and their military exploits, the arches served as emblems of power for the ancient Romans.

LEFT: Palace Square in St. Petersburg, Russia, is decorated with a triumphal arch topped by bronze statues depicting soldiers and a parade of horses. Similar sculpture groups topped the arches of ancient Rome.

RIGHT: Atop the Winter Palace in St. Petersburg, a crowned double-headed eagle stands as a symbol of Russian imperial power.

The Column

Like the triumphal arch, the column is an ancient Roman invention that was borrowed and reinterpreted by subsequent leaders. The Column of Trajan was erected in Rome in about A.D. 113 It marked the center of a square flanked by great libraries holding Greek and Latin texts that were built under the emperor Trajan's reign. After the emperor's death in A.D. 117, a golden urn containing his ashes was placed inside the giant base of the column. The impressive marble column measures 125 feet (38 meters) high, and originally displayed a bronze statue of Trajan. A spiral band of relief sculpture from the base to the tip of the column narrates the military exploits of the emperor's troops with thousands of writhing figures, animals, and battle scenes sculpted in marble. If it were possible to roll out the spiraling scenes like a scroll, it would measure more than 650 feet (198 meters) long.

Seventeen centuries later, the column form still conveyed meaning for British society. In Trafalgar Square in the heart of London, Nelson's Column stands 145 feet (44 meters) high. Like the Column of Trajan, Nelson's Column commemorates a great military victory, in this case the naval battle at Trafalgar in 1805. In the Roman tradition, Nelson's Column marks the center of an important city square, stands atop a large pedestal, and bears a sculpture of the leader. The monument was designed by William Raiton between 1838 and 1842, and was topped by sculptor Edward Hodges Baily's realistic depiction of Lord Nelson, who lost an eye and an arm in battle.

LEFT: The relief work on Trajan's Column, which stands in the Forum of Trajan in Rome, commemorates that Roman emperor's victories in the Dacian Wars (A.D. 102 and 105).

LEFT: The relief sculptures on the base of Nelson's Column in London commemorate the British naval victory in the Battle of Trafalgar of 1805.

FOLLOWING PAGE: Rostzal Column in St. Petersburg, Russia, provides another example of the endurance of the monumental column in different countries throughout the world. The ancient Romans first used such columns to glorify their rulers.

LEFT: The 145-foot (44-meter) Nelson's Column marks the center of London's Trafalgar Square. The rectangular base supports a fluted column that is in turn topped by a statue of Lord Nelson.

The Wall

Throughout history, walls have had a common purpose—to keep people within them safe and to keep those outside them at bay. In fact, the wall is symbol of civilization itself. The earliest civilized settlements at Jericho, in modern-day Jordan, were surrounded by high walls as early as 7000 B.C. Nearly all towns during the middle ages were encircled by extensive walls, complete with elaborate defensive towers, arrow slits, and openings through which to dump hot oil or steaming water on would-be attackers. The wall is a symbol of civilization, of war, of protection, and of power.

Constructed under the Roman emperor Hadrian in the mid-second century A.D., Hadrian's Wall snakes across narrowest part of England from the Solway firth to the Tyne River. The emperor intended the giant barrier to be the permanent northern frontier of the Roman empire. The Romans saw the peoples to the north, in what is present-day Scotland, as a barbaric and uncivilized lot who were not worth fighting and best sealed off from the more sophisticated Roman-British culture that occupied the rest of the island. It is not surprising that, at 80 miles (129 kilometers) long, at least 8 feet (2.5 meters) thick,

LEFT: The Great Wall of China sprawls some 1,500 miles (2,414 kilometers) across the Asian continent. The emperor Shih Huang Pi began this incredible project in the fifth century B.C. in order to keep would-be invaders at bay. A turret in one of its towers provides a dramatic vista onto the wall's expanse.

ABOVE: Now a rambling ruin set against a pastoral, green landscape near the border of England and Scotland, Hadrian's Wall was once the first line of defense for the ancient Romans who occupied these lands in the second century A.D.

and 15 feet (4.5 meters) high, much of Hadrian's Wall survives today. Modern visitors can walk along the various well-preserved sections of the wall and observe the fascinating ruins of Roman military outposts along the way.

But even Hadrian's impressive wall pales in the face of the Great Wall of China. Standing more than 20 feet (6 meters) tall, 13 feet (4 meters) wide, and made of earth, rubble, and masonry, the Great Wall winds 1,500 miles (2,413 kilometers) through valleys, rivers, and mountains. It stretches almost halfway across modern China from the Yellow Sea to the Gobi Desert. The wall was begun under Emperor Shih Huang Pi in the fifth century B.C., but was not completed until the Ming Dynasty. Like Hadrian's Wall in Britain, the Great Wall of China was intended to keep marauding nomads to the north at bay, in this case the peoples inhabiting Mongolia. The Great Wall is sometimes called the Eighth Wonder of the World, and astronauts say that it is one of the only manmade structures on earth that can be seen from the moon.

Probably the most well-known wall of the twentieth century is the Berlin Wall. In 1961, after about 160,000 refugees had fled East Germany for western countries, the East German government erected the wall to halt the flow of its people. Though it is referred to as a single entity, the Berlin Wall was actually a series of solid barriers, barbed wire, and open areas lit with flood lamps and pierced with guard towers. At least one hundred people were killed trying to cross the wall between 1961 and 1989. In 1989, emboldened by the rapidly changing political climate, East Berliners began to dismantle the wall. By 1990, the wall had been destroyed almost entirely with pickaxes, tanks, and other tools. Only a few sections remain today, a token reminder of the once-formidable barrier measuring more than 103 miles (166 kilometers). The historic Brandenburg Gate in East Berlin, built in 1791 as a symbol of peace, once again fulfilled its mission as a place of celebration during the Wall's destruction. A new monument memorializing the fall of the Berlin Wall was constructed in 1992.

LEFT: The Winter Palace in St. Petersburg, Russia, stands as a grandiose backdrop for the Alexander Column in Palace Square, erected to celebrate Russia's defeat of Napoleon in 1812 under Tsar Alexander I.

RIGHT: When the Brandenburg Gate was originally erected in Berlin in 1791, it stood as a symbol of peace. Today, it symbolizes peace once again after twenty-eight years of enclosure behind the Berlin Wall. The wall itself symbolized freedom and resistance to oppression for many in the West until its destruction in 1989.

Regal Residences

The abodes of heads of state and religious leaders count among the most impressive monuments in the world. With their imposing scale and usually ostentatious decoration, these structures are meant to impress. In most cases, these buildings are monuments within monuments—they encompass statues, fountains, gardens, and other structures within the overall design of the residence. At the Escorial, situated in the rugged plains north of Madrid, cold gray stones mask an interior of magnificent luxury. This vast sixteenth-century complex, the brainchild of King Philip II, encompasses a monastery, library,

BELOW: The Escorial (1563–84) was originally built by Philip II as a monastery commemorating the Spanish victory over the French at Saint-Quentin in 1557.

two pantheons, and two palaces. Likewise, the Schönnbrun in Vienna is a sumptuous baroque palace that served as the summer residence of the Hapsburgs. It includes 1,441 rooms and the oldest zoo in Europe, dating from 1752.

Though it is set in Rome, Vatican City is just that— an autonomous city both politically and architecturally. The Vatican encompasses sprawling buildings of many eras. The cavernous basilica of St. Peter sits at the heart of Vatican City, supplanting an early Christian basilica. The colonnade, built by Gianlorenzo Bernini in the seventeenth century, embraces crowds of the faithful in the forecourt of the basilica. The Sistine Chapel, the Pope's residence, the Vatican Library, and a host of other administrative buildings round out the complex.

Versailles, the royal palace that sprawls just outside of Paris, is probably the most ostentatious residence of any European

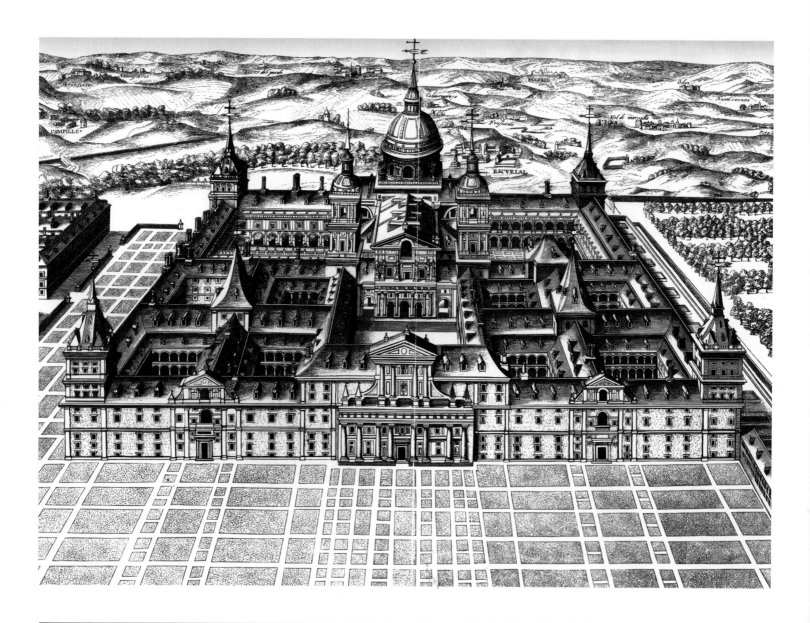

ABOVE: These golden gates mark the entrance to the château of Versailles, just outside of Paris. French king Louis XIV reigned from this luxurious palace from 1682 to 1715 and it was occupied by his heirs until the French Revolution.

LEFT: The Schönnbrun Palace in Vienna, Austria, was the summer residence of the Hapsburg kings and their courts. Its imposing Baroque façade and geometric gardens recall the similar effect at Versailles.

The expansive symmetrical gardens are just one of the wonders of the royal palace of Versailles. One wing of the château serves as a backdrop for the park-like grounds, which include not only gardens, but numerous fountains, ponds, and topiary formations.

king in history. The architects Louis Le Vau and Jules Hardouin-Mansart began the design in 1669, but the embellishment of Versailles continued through the end of the century. Louis XIV was known as the Sun King and associated himself with the ancient god Apollo, and he dictated that all of the château's decoration must relate to the sun and Apollo. Avenues and garden paths radiate outward from the palace like rays of the sun and gilded fountains and their sculptures depict Apollo driving his chariot across the sky. The château of Versailles encompasses suites for the royal family and its entourage, state rooms, ballrooms, and one of the most extravagant systems of parks, gardens, fountains, and forests in the world.

On a more modest scale, the White House, besides being home to the president of the United States, also contains the Oval Office and various state rooms, parlors, and private suites on six floors. James Hoban designed the building at 1600 Pennsylvania Avenue, and its classical columns and stark white façade make it immediately recognizable. Work began on the building in 1792, and although George Washington oversaw the construction, he never lived there; John Adams, the second president of the United States, was the first to live in the White House. British troops set fire to the White House in 1814. The outside was saved, but it took three years to rebuild the inside. Before 1907, when President Theodore Roosevelt gave the house its official name, it was known as the President's Palace, the President's House, and the Executive Mansion. Until the Civil War, it was the biggest house in the United States.

LEFT: The White House in Washington, D.C., was begun in 1792. John Adams, the second president of the United States, was its first resident. The building has only been officially called the White House since 1907.

LEFT: At Sans Souci Palace in Potsdam, Germany, delicate sculptures ornament the exterior of this building, built in the mid-eighteenth century by Frederick the Great.

Statues of Stature

A statue is the most common type of monument, and since the beginning of recorded history rulers have recognized the commemorative and propagandistic potential of statues. While statues of national leaders are perhaps the most common, statues of local heroes and heroines also adorn city squares across the world. A statue of Joan of Arc marks the center of the Place du Martroi in Orléans, the French city liberated by Joan of Arc in 1429 after a seven-month siege by English invaders.

In an equestrian statue, which depicts a ruler on horseback, the hero is both literally and symbolically elevated above the people. The second-century A.D. equestrian statue of Marcus Aurelius in Rome depicts the emperor sitting proudly astride his horse, raising his hand toward the people. It is the only bronze statue of a ruler on horseback to survive from antiquity. The statue survived the middle ages—a period that witnessed the wholesale melting of metal statues of the ancient pagan world—because it was believed to be an image of Constantine, the first Christian emperor.

The popularity of equestrian statues was revived in the Renaissance and continued in subsequent centuries. The equestrian statue of the Russian czar Peter the Great stands in the square alongside the Senate in St. Petersburg, Russia. Peter the Great was responsible for building the beautiful city of St. Petersburg, called the Venice of the North and later known as Leningrad, in the seventeenth and eighteenth centuries. In 1782, the French sculptor Etienne Falconet executed the larger-than-life-size image of the czar, riding competently astride a rearing horse with the laurel wreath of victory on his head. Falconet used horses in the royal stable as models for his dramatic monument.

LEFT: This majestic statue of Joan of Arc in Orléans shows the medieval French heroine sitting astride her horse, ready to lead her city to freedom.

RIGHT: A statue of Peter the Great in St. Petersburg, Russia depicts the ruler in a dynamic, active pose. Erected by Empress Catherine the Great, it stood even during the Communist era as a symbol of Russian national pride and patriotism.

FRIEDRICH DEM GROSSEN
FRIEDRICH WILHELM DER DRITTE
MDCCCXXXX
VOLLENDET UNTER FRIEDR WILH DEM VIERTEN
MDCCCLI

BELOW: In Bruges, a statue of Jan Breydel and Pieter De Coninck commemorates the role of these two revolutionary Belgian citizens in the battle against French dictators in 1302.

ABOVE: An early engraving depicts one of the obelisks called Cleopatra's Needle, from the ancient Egyptian city of Heliopolis, famous as the center of sun worship and for its schools of philosophy and astronomy.

LEFT: In Berlin, a statue of Frederick II of Germany stands majestically above his subjects. The equestrian statue, in which a ruler is depicted on horseback, literally "above" the people, has been a standard way of depicting rulers since ancient times.

Monuments in the Mountainside

The majestic portraits of four American presidents protruding from Mount Rushmore, in the Black Hills of South Dakota, were the brainchild of the sculptor Gutzon Borglum. The son of Danish immigrants and a student of the French sculptor Auguste Rodin, Borglum began the project in 1927; it took him fourteen years to finish the work while he raised funds from private donors and eventually from the federal government. The likeness of American presidents George Washington, Thomas Jefferson, Theodore Roosevelt, and Abraham Lincoln were carved into the mountain of granite with the aid of jackhammers and dynamite. Originally, Borglum envisioned that the figures would be shown from the head to the waistline, but the sculptor died before completing the project. Today, visitors marvel at the 60-foot (18-meter) high faces—a shrine to democracy and the unique vision of the artist some 500 feet (153 meters) above the ground.

Like Mount Rushmore, Stone Mountain, outside of Atlanta, Georgia, has portraits carved into its face. Stone Mountain is the largest single piece of granite on earth and a perfectly smooth surface, so it seems a likely location for relief sculpture. The image depicts three Civil War leaders on horseback, shown in profile—Thomas J. "Stonewall" Jackson, General Robert E. Lee, and Confederate president Jefferson Davis. The state of Georgia has operated the surrounding park since 1958 as a monument to the Confederacy, and the carving was completed 1972. The relief sits 400 feet (122 meters) above ground, is recessed 42 feet (13 meters) into the mountain, and measures 90 by 190 feet (27 by 58 meters). It is the largest relief sculpture in the world.

LEFT: American Civil War leaders Stonewall Jackson, Robert E. Lee, and Jefferson Davis appear in the largest relief sculpture in the world, the Confederate Memorial sculpted into the side of Stone Mountain, near Atlanta, Georgia.

ABOVE: As the sun rises at Mount Rushmore in the Black Hills of South Dakota, the monumental faces of American presidents George Washington, Thomas Jefferson, Theodore Roosevelt, and Abraham Lincoln emerge.

CHAPTER THREE

MEMORIALS

The tomb is probably the world's oldest type of monument. In ancient Egypt, the tomb and its accouterments helped the deceased prepare for life beyond the grave. In modern times, grave markers establish the location where someone is buried after death, and in many cases celebrate the deceased's life through words and images. Cemeteries boast some of the world's most important monuments. Arlington National Cemetery in Virginia possesses the remains of America's presidents and heroes; the Valley of the Kings in Egypt commemorates the pharaohs; Westminster Abbey contains a memorial to great English writers; and Père Lachaise cemetery in Paris contains the bodies and memorials of some of the most important writers and artists of the nineteenth and twentieth centuries.

The word "memorial" usually brings to mind the commemoration of the deceased, usually national heroes or victims of war or other large-scale disasters. Memorials are often collective, as in the memorial to victims of the confrontation between the Russian Parliament and President Boris Yeltsin in October of 1993. Other memorials are dedicated to the memory of individuals. There are numerous memorials to Dr. Martin Luther King across the United States, including the King Mural at the King Memorial Library in Washington, D.C., and the King Center in Atlanta, Georgia.

Monumental Leaders

The mall in Washington, D.C., is home to many of America's greatest monuments. The Lincoln Memorial, which commemorates President Abraham Lincoln, uses a classical design to convey the grandeur of the leader. As he constructed the Lincoln Memorial between 1914 and 1922, the architect Henry Bacon exploited the symbolic potential of the design. The thirty-six Doric columns represent the thirty-six states that existed at the

RIGHT: The Lincoln Memorial, the Washington Memorial, and the Capitol building are just three of the many monuments that adorn the Mall in Washington, D.C.

LEFT: At the Church of the Dome at the Hôtel des Invalides in Paris, designed by the architect Jules Hardouin-Mansart in 1676–1706, the exterior dome is embellished with gold. The church houses the remains of the emperor Napoleon I, as well as such French military figures as Vauban, Turenne, and Foch, whose statue is on the left.

BELOW: The tomb of the emperor Napoleon Bonaparte, in the Church of the Dome in Paris, is made of red porphyry. Within, Napoleon's body is encased in a series of six coffins.

time of Lincoln's assassination in Ford's Theater in 1865. The frieze enumerates the forty-eight states that existed at the time the memorial was constructed. Stone from all over the nation—Colorodo Yule marble for the exterior, Massachusetts granite for the walkway, Indiana limestone for the interior walls, and Tennessee pink marble for the floor—further contributes to the symbolism of the monument. Just as Lincoln sought to unite the war-torn states, the monument uses marble from every corner of the country. In rendering the likeness of Lincoln, the sculptor Daniel Chester French wanted to convey Lincoln's confidence and mental strength in bringing the American Civil War to completion in the pose, the gesture of the hands, and the facial expression. Because French never saw Lincoln in person (Lincoln had died some six decades earlier), the sculptor relied on old photographs and a life mask of Lincoln's face cast by the sculptor Leonard Volk in 1860. It took French four years to achieve these qualities of solidity and intensity in the impressive seated statue of America's sixteenth president.

Like the Lincoln Memorial, the Jefferson Memorial uses a classical vocabulary to convey the sense of grandeur and idealism associated with Thomas Jefferson, the third president of the United States and the writer of the Declaration of

LEFT: The stolid face of American President Abraham Lincoln gazes out from the impressive Lincoln Memorial in Washington, D.C. The sculptor Daniel Chester French relied on old photographs and a mask of Lincoln's face in creating this likeness.

Independence. Jefferson is seen as the philosopher behind the American Revolution, and the walls of the Memorial are inscribed with his writings. In designing the Memorial, the architect John Russell Pope was inspired by Jefferson's well-known classical architectural tastes. Like Jefferson's home in Monticello, Virginia, the Memorial is based on the Pantheon in Rome, with an interior dome of recessed cells. As in the Lincoln Memorial, the Jefferson Memorial uses a variety of marbles from different parts of the country. The monument was completed between 1938 and 1943. The 19-foot (5.8 meter), 5-ton bronze statue of Jefferson seems to gaze toward the White House. President Franklin D. Roosevelt had trees removed from the grounds of the Memorial when it was completed in order to afford a better view from the presidential residence.

The burial places of great leaders often are marked by notable monuments, such as the reserved, classical tomb of Napoleon Bonaparte, designed by Visconti. Today, Napoleon's tomb stands in Paris under the dome of Les Invalides, a church designed by the architect Jules Hardouin-Mansart between 1676 and 1706 as part of a home for disabled veterans established under King Louis XIV. Although Napoleon had been buried on the island of St. Helena in 1821, King Louis-Philippe of France arranged to have the emperor's remains repatriated to France in 1840 after seven years of negotiation with the British government. The coffin was exhumed and opened for two minutes, and those who viewed the body claimed that it remained uncorrupted. The remains were transported on a frigate via the Seine River to Paris, where a majestic parade proceeded up the Champs-Elysées past Napoleon's most well-known monument, the Arc de Triomphe. After an official state funeral, the new tomb was placed in the crypt below the dome of the church of Les Invalides, a stone's throw from the army parade field where Napoleon had been a cadet some half a century earlier.

Perhaps the best known tombs of rulers are the Great Pyramids of Giza, built about 2500 B.C. in a location 8 miles (13 kilometers) outside of Cairo. In ancient Egypt, giant pyramids were seen as a fitting burial place for a king. The pyramids of three Egyptian pharaohs—Cheops, Chephren, and Mycerinus—dominate the arid desert with their impressive scale and absolute simplicity. The largest pyramid, that of Cheops, dominates the others at more than 480 feet (146 meters) high. Smaller pyramids for other royal family members stand nearby. Perfect isosceles triangles form the four sides of the pyramids, which were originally faced with smooth limestone that has crumbled away over the intervening centuries. How did the ancient Egyptians, to whom the wheel was unknown, move these giant stones? The huge limestone blocks were probably brought by boat from other side of the Nile and rolled on logs up brick ramps, where they were slid into place.

LEFT: At the Jefferson Memorial in Washington, D.C., the classical tastes of America's third president were harnessed by the architect John Russell Pope. The building was inspired by the ancient Pantheon of Rome, but is constructed with marbles from many regions of the United States.

RIGHT: In the Jefferson Memorial, the statue of the president is surrounded by inscriptions taken from the president's own writings. The statue is positioned so that Jefferson appears to gaze toward the White House.

I HAVE SWORN U

WE HOLD THESE TRUTHS TO BE SELF-
EVIDENT: THAT ALL MEN ARE CREATED
EQUAL, THAT THEY ARE ENDOWED BY THEIR
CREATOR WITH CERTAIN INALIENABLE
RIGHTS, AMONG THESE ARE LIFE, LIBERTY
AND THE PURSUIT OF HAPPINESS, THAT
TO SECURE THESE RIGHTS GOVERNMENTS
ARE INSTITUTED AMONG MEN. WE···
SOLEMNLY PUBLISH AND DECLARE, THAT
THESE COLONIES ARE AND OF RIGHT
OUGHT TO BE FREE AND INDEPENDENT
STATES···AND FOR THE SUPPORT OF THIS
DECLARATION, WITH A FIRM RELIANCE
ON THE PROTECTION OF DIVINE
PROVIDENCE, WE MUTUALLY PLEDGE
OUR LIVES, OUR FORTUNES AND OUR
SACRED HONOUR.

BELOW: Like the Taj Mahal, the Albert Memorial is a tribute to a beloved royal consort. After Prince Albert's untimely death at age forty-two, for the rest of her life Queen Victoria dressed in mourning for her husband. The memorial stands in a park facing London's Albert Hall.

ABOVE: Old Quebec City in Canada proudly displays a statue honoring Samuel de Champlain (1567–1635), the French explorer who founded, governed, and watched over the colony that was to become the city of Quebec.

LEFT: Shown here is the King's Pantheon from the Escorial near Madrid, part of a vast complex of buildings including a monastery, church, royal palace, mausoleum, college, and library.

ABOVE: At Juno Beach in Normandy, one of many D-Day memorials commemorates the day when Allied forces landed on these beaches in 1944 to liberate Europe during World War II.

BELOW: An Allied forces tank-turned-memorial graces Juno Beach in Normandy, France, the site of the Allied invasion that marked the beginning of the end of World War II.

Sites of Conflict

Battlegrounds are often honored as monuments. Gettysburg, Pennsylvania, was one of the bloodiest sites of the American Civil War and is today visited by thousands each year. An eloquent poem by Lieutenant Colonel John McCrae memorializes Flanders Field in Belgium, the site of the World War I battle of Ypres in the spring of 1915. Today, the beaches of Normandy boast numerous museums, memorials, and cemeteries commemorating the landing of American and British troops in France in June of 1944 and the subsequent battles in the region.

"Remember the Alamo!" is the cry of those recalling the battle of the Alamo in San Antonio, Texas, along the Mexican-American border. The battle of the Alamo lasted thirteen days in 1836, when 189 Texas volunteers defended the site against four thousand Mexican troops led by the self-proclaimed dictator Santa Ana. Although all the American defenders lost their lives, including the legendary Davy Crockett, the battle of the Alamo is celebrated as the moment when Texas won its independence. The state was annexed by the United States nine years later. Some remains on the site today actually predate the battle of the Alamo, and consist of a chapel and a fortress erected by the Spanish when they established a mission there in the eighteenth century. The building that now stands was begun about 1755, and is a prime example of Spanish colonial architecture. Since 1905, the Alamo has been administered by the Daughters of the Republic of Texas, and today includes a shrine, museums, a theater, and a library.

RIGHT: The Alamo in San Antonio, Texas, began as a Spanish mission, but became the site of a bloody battle and a symbol of Texas independence from Mexico. The façade of the eighteenth-century Spanish missionaries' church is an excellent example of Spanish colonial architecture in the New World.

LEFT: The barrel-vaulted interior of the memorial at Verdun, France, contains memorials to those who lost their lives in World War I.

RIGHT: Of the once-imposing church dedicated to Kaiser Wilhelm I in Berlin, a bell tower is all that remains, a poignant reminder of war's destructive capabilities.

LEFT: In Verdun, France, the countless graves of fallen soldiers make for a sobering reminder of the consequences of World War I. A memorial erected by Americans silently watches over the graves.

Monuments to War Veterans

Monuments to war veterans are among the most poignant memorials in the world. Many countries, including the United States, Britain, and France, have a Tomb of the Unknown Soldier, a symbolic way of honoring the sacrifice of the many unidentified soldiers who have sacrificed their lives for their countries. The Marine Corps Memorial in Washington, D.C., better known as the Iwo Jima statue, is a cast bronze statue dedicated to all American Marines who have lost their lives since 1775. The USS *Arizona* is a memorial to the 1,177 crewmen who perished on the naval vessel during the Japanese attack on Pearl Harbor, Hawaii, on December 7, 1941. A reinforced concrete structure was erected on pilings between 1960 and 1962 to mark the spot above the submerged ship, but the sunken ship itself is the memorial.

Among the most recent war memorials in the United States is the Vietnam Veterans Memorial on the mall in Washington, D.C., better known as "the wall." The monument consists of two long walls made of polished black granite placed together in a chevron pattern; one points toward the Washington Monument and the other toward the Lincoln Memorial. The names of the 59,196 men and women who died in Southeast Asia between 1959 and 1975, or who are still missing, are listed chronologically in the order in which they were lost. The wall thus serves

ABOVE: The Marine Corps Memorial in Washington, D.C., is better known as the "Iwo Jima Statue." The cast bronze monument memorializes all American Marines who gave their lives, and depicts a poignant moment when soldiers struggled to erect the flag on the battlefield.

ABOVE: This realistic sculptural group stands alongside the more abstract Vietnam War Memorial in Washington, D.C. The three soldiers seem to be reading the long list of names inscribed on the wall designed by Maya Lin in 1982.

LEFT: The Tomb of the Unknown Soldier in Arlington National Cemetery in Arlington, Virginia, is one of many such memorials in countries around the world.

as both a collective and an individual tribute. A twenty-one-year-old architecture student from Yale University, Maya Yin Lin, won a design competition for the memorial, which was built in 1982. Like the Vietnam War itself, the monument was controversial. Some veterans' groups objected to the abstract nature of the monument, and in 1984, Frederick Hart's *Statue of Three Servicemen* was added. This bronze statue realistically depicts three soldiers of various races and branches of the armed services; they seem to be looking toward the great wall of names. Today, the Vietnam Veterans Memorial is the most visited of all the National Park Service sites in Washington, D.C.

In addition to collective war memorials, many lesser-known monuments honor specific accomplishments and sacrifices of particular soldiers. The Robert Gould Shaw and 54th Regiment Memorial, located on Boston Common in Boston, Massachusetts, commemorates the 54th Regiment of the Massachusetts Volunteer Infantry, the first black regiment in the north to fight in the American Civil War. President Abraham Lincoln granted the regiment a place in the Union army in 1863, and Robert Gould Shaw, a white officer, volunteered to command the regiment. The life-size relief sculpture, facing the State House on Boston Common, commemorates the assault on Fort Wagner in an attempt to capture Charleston, South Carolina. Sergeant William Carney, wounded while saving the American flag from capture by Confederate forces, was the first African American to be awarded a Congressional Medal of Honor.

ABOVE: This war memorial in Kuala Lumpur, Malaysia, depicts soldiers in active, dynamic poses, expressing the chaos and violence of battle.

ABOVE: A World War I monument in Inverary, Argyl, Scotland, pays homage to those who died in battle in the service of their country.

PHILIP HOWELL · DALE P HUDSON · JULIO E MORALES-GONZALEZ · PAUL E HURDEL · LEROY WILLIAMS ·
ALPHA R JACKSON · DEAN A JACKSON · JAMES C JACKSON · GERALD A KOSAKOWSKI · HARRY F JEDRZEJEWSKI ·
FRED H JENKINS · WILBERT H JOHNSON · CECIL W KITTLE Jr · MARTIN C KNAPP · THOMAS JAMES ·
DUNCAN F KRUEGER · RAMON KUILAN-OLIVERAS · JOSEPH S LA FASO · GARRETT F LEE · WILLIAM J LINDSEY ·
VINCENT LOCATELLI · HENRY T LUNA · WAY E T LUNDELL · JACK D LYNN · RONALD R MARTIN · JAMES A GILFORD ·
RONNIE T MATHIS · DAVID L MENDOZA · NALD A MILLER · PALMER B MILES · MICHAEL J MILLER ·
ROGER E MERCK · MALCOLM E MILLICAN · YD J MONSEWICZ · ARTHUR R MOODY III · CHARLES T MOORE Jr ·
CARL M HUME · ROBERT MORENO · GLEN T McCAMMON · HAROLD D McCARN · PREZEL McCULLOUGH ·
GEORGE S McHELLON · JIMMY D NAKAYA. ROGER T NELSON · ROY L RYSE Jr · THEOPHILOS ORPHANOS ·
SHERMAN E OTIS · RICHARD D OTT · ISMA PAREDES · AUGUSTIN CHAVEZ PAREDEZ · DONALD C PETERSON ·
THOMAS C PIZZINO · WILLIAM A PLEASAN ROBERT POSIUS · LOUIS D RICHARDSON · HOWARD G RILEY ·
JESSE N RODRIGUEZ · CLAYTON G ROGER FRANK J NOSTADT Jr · DARRELL W SANDERS · RICHARD P SAWICKI ·
GUY L SCHAEFFER · MURVIN SCHALIPP Jr IN SCHLECHT III · JERROLD J SCHLIESMAN · EUGENE C SCOTT ·
HAROLD SCOTT · JOHN A SHAW · MATTH SHELTON · ROBERT S SHRIVER Jr · EDWARD L SIMMONS ·
ROGER A SIMRAU · GARY D SMITH · HENR SMITH · MICHAEL T SMITH · SIDNEY C M SMITH · JOSEPH A FORD III ·
NORMAN W SOLTOW · CHARLES T STEINE GEORGE J STEPHENS · ROGER A STONE · CHARLES W STOREY ·
FINIS R STUDDARD · ERNEST E TAYLOR · JE TAYLOR · ROBERT E WALDVOGEL · EARTHELL TYLER ·
GEORGE A WILSON · JAMES O VAUGHAN GUEL DE JESUS VERA-DURAN · BOBBY C VINSON · PAUL E TOLBERT ·
MACK A WARE · NEOPOLIS WIGFALL · DAV VANCELLETTE · FRED D WITCHET · JOHN H WOODY ·
JOSEPH M WORKMAN · ROBERT G WRIGH GORDON P YOUNG · RICHARD T YOUNG · BENJIMAN BROOKS ·
● RONALD H CHITTUM · RICHARD C CLAI NDSEY H CROW · LOUIS S GUTIERREZ · JOHN F McDERMOTT ·
PAUL H EKLUND · ARLIN R JENSEN · RAY ON · DAVID L REEDER · EVERETT B THOMPSON · FELIX RODRIQUEZ ·
FRANK D TRYPUS · DAVID L VARVELL · R D BALMER · RICHARD D BRODA · CONNIE L CHANDLER ·
JOHN P EMERLING · ANDRE HAROULAK ALD P JOHNSON · JOSEPH P MARA · GEORGE McCUTCHEN ·
IVAN NOTEBOOM · DONALD H PERRIG NNETH E SARGENT · JOSE W SUAREZ · WILLIAM J TAYLOR III ·
BILLY JOE WILSON · OSCAR E COOPER ANCIS Jr · WALTER C MILLER · KENNETH POLING ·
DENNIS L TOMS · BARRY F ANDERSEN A BERINGER · RICHARD R BIGLEY · GUST CALLIVAS ·
JOHN D CAMPBELL · RAYMOND CELES S E DOUGLAS · DARELL G FREEMAN · KENNETH J HAMMO ·
BILLY W HEDGE · VILIS LISMENTS · RIC ER · VICTOR J PIRKER · MOSES C TABOR ROBERT M THROPE ·
FRANCIS E VISCONTI · RICHARD G W WINKLER · TERRY WINTERMOYER · THEODORE M BEAMON ·
DAVID GUERRERO BENAVENTE · LC E G BRITTEN · JOHN V FIORENTIN · RICHARD E G RGE ·
GUNDER P R GUNDERSON · GERALD HARD JENSEN · GLENN D MANN · DAVID W MICHAEL ·
ROBIN A RARIG · CLEO SMITH · DANI SAMMY LEE THOMPSON · TERRY LEE BIX ·
JOHNNY W BOUINGTON · NATHAN DALE L FUNK · ARTHUR M GORDON ·
LESTER KEY · RONALD J LOERLEIN · W EN · DONALD R BONKO ORT DAVIS ·
DENNIS L LONG · DENNIS F AMATO MAN · JOHN M GRASSO PH ·
LESTER J KERSTEN · GUY H McCAREY ELY · TONY VALE LES GRA WE ·
ROBERT W ANDREASEN · MORRIS L I GREEN · VIRGIL D MICH ·
RALPH G HAMLIN Jr · GEORGE L STO BECKER · TYRONE L STEP ·
KENNETH M JACKSON · JOHN V McCO USTIN · THOMA ARN RO ·
● ARTHUR N McMELLON · MORRIS E JE GAN · GERALD R ERTS ● RAY ·
RAFAEL ACEVEDO-RECHANI · PETER N RD W MILLER LEY G JO ·
WARREN L DEMPSEY · WILLIAM R McI FY · RO A S RHOUSE ·
ROBERT H WHITE · LAWRENCE G BRO HER ES DA-COSTAS ·
TOM W BROWN · STANLEY L SAPP · K DO ·
JAMES A WATSON · DOUGLAS V AND DAVID L ·
MORRIS F DIBBLE · GEORGE J B EISEN FACONDIN ·
JAMES GRAHAM · JOHN P GREENE · JIMMY DO ·
NORMAN W JOHNSON · JERRY B JO LE R JONES ·
RAYMOND E KELLEMS · RICHARD KI NG · CZESLA OW ·
O'NEAL LEGETTE · McGEA TTLE J EN · ROBERT D LOGUE ·
JAMES E LOVE · CHARLES E ZAN MARSH · DONALD W M ·
WARREN S OSHIRO · JOSEP IG Jr · CARLOS HERIBE TO RU ARTHY ·
MILTON SOLOMON · NOR G R W SPRADLIN · DON G STALLA RT ·
JOHN L THIBEAULT · HARRY S ON TUNGATE · EDWARD C UPNER · V ·
DANIEL A DICKINSON · HERBER H DAY ORN · WILLIAM M MEGLIO EZA ·
PAUL A ROBERTSON · JOHN T ST HN W EDE Jr THOMAS P LAVIN · JAM

3
E

4
E

Marines

ANTHO
PETER M
EDMUN
ROY S K
ALBERT
CHARLE
JOHNNI
JOSEPH
CHARLE
EDWARI
W D HU
EDWARD
EDWARD
BOBBIE
ERIC SA
FRANK V
GEORGE
ARTHUR
CAREY E
● HUGHLE
JOHN M
WILBUR
CARLOS
HARRY M
JAMES R
CHARLES
FLOYD A
ROY F B
JESSE L H
HAROLD
MICHAE
PAUL R L
EVERETT
ELMER J
ST EY
BERT
RAY
JOHN J
VICTOR
CHARLES
CLAREN
RODNEY
N R S
DAVID B
JACK W
RUSSELL
DODD
KALE R
JESSE T B
DAVID A
MICHAE
ROBERT
RONALD

LEFT: The Vietnam War Memorial in Washington, D.C., consists of a monolithic wall inscribed with thousands of names representing soldiers killed or missing in action during the Vietnam War.

LEFT: Arlington National Cemetery in Virginia, across the Potomac River from Washington, D.C., honors many thousands of war dead as well as notable Americans such as former President John F. Kennedy. The site also includes the Tomb of the Unknown Soldier.

RIGHT: At this war memorial in Melbourne, Australia, the understated classical façade and sober exterior lend a sense of solemnity and grandeur.

Memorial to War Victims

In addition to memorials to soldiers, memorials to war victims are also found throughout the world. World War II, which claimed the lives of millions of civilians, counts among its many memorials three poignant monuments that commemorate its innocent victims. The Peace Park in Hiroshima, Japan, was erected to commemorate the victims of the first atomic bomb ever dropped on a city on August 6, 1945. The A-bomb, dispatched from the aircraft *Enola Gay*, fell on central Hiroshima, leveling ninety percent of the city and claiming as many as 200,000 lives. The Peace Park is a complex of monuments erected in an area of the city gutted by the bomb. The landscaped park contains personalized memorials to children, fountains, bells, a clock tower, a memorial to Korean victims of the A-bomb, and other monuments. It also houses a collection of items and objects that survived the explosion.

Like the Peace Park of Hiroshima, the Holocaust Memorial in Jerusalem, Israel, is a complex of monuments within a larger framework. The memorial is located on the Mount of Remembrance in Jerusalem, and commemorates the victims of the Holocaust from 1933 to 1945 under the Nazi regime of Germany, whose lethal ideology led to the mass murder of Jews as part of Adolf Hitler's "Final Solution." The Holocaust Memorial encompasses a complex of museums, monuments, a library, archives, museums, a memorial to Jewish children, and other resource centers.

LEFT: The war memorial at Hiroshima, Japan, is a sobering reminder of the dropping of the Atomic Bomb in 1945. Today, the "Peace Park" contains numerous memorials to the victims of the bomb.

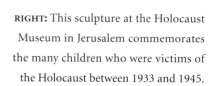

RIGHT: This sculpture at the Holocaust Museum in Jerusalem commemorates the many children who were victims of the Holocaust between 1933 and 1945.

RIGHT: Outside the Russian Museum in St. Petersburg stands a statue commemorating Alexandr Sergeyevich Pushkin (1799–1837), the poet and prose writer among the foremost figures in Russian literature.

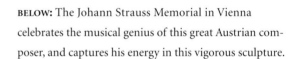

BELOW: Flowers in the form of a treble clef stand before the delicately carved memorial to Wolfgang Amadeus Mozart in Vienna, Austria, the city of some of the composer's greatest successes.

BELOW: The Johann Strauss Memorial in Vienna celebrates the musical genius of this great Austrian composer, and captures his energy in this vigorous sculpture.

A Memorial to Love

The Taj Mahal, the famous monument in Agra, India, was constructed between 1630 and 1648 by Shah Jahan, the Muslim leader of India, as memorial to his favorite wife, Mumtaz Mahal. The overall effect of the Taj Mahal is one of complete tranquillity. Although its bulbous dome stands more than 250 feet (76 meters) high, the entire structure appears weightless and light, translucent and elegant. The sheer white marble surfaces of the building shimmer in the reflecting pool, glowing under the balloon-like dome. Arabic inscriptions describe paradisiacal gardens, much like the sumptuous gardens that surround the domed mausoleum with its four minarets. At his death, Shah Jahan was interred there alongside his wife.

Preserving the Past for the Future

Are monuments only a thing of the past? Not if the surprisingly large number of new monuments that are built throughout the world every year continues to grow. In the early 1990s, more than eighty new monument proposals were under consideration in Washington, D.C., alone. It seems that monument building is more vital than ever.

ABOVE: The Taj Mahal in Agra, India, stands like a mirage, its reflection mirrored in the still waters before it. The elegant building was constructed in 1630–48 by Shah Jahan, the Muslim leader of India, as a memorial to his favorite wife, Mumtaz Mahal.

We think of monuments as enduring, everlasting, and permanent—as indeed they are meant to be. But many of the world's greatest monuments are in peril. During the last fifty years, pollution has devastated the world's monuments. The ancient Greek sculptures of the Parthenon in Athens face destruction from the harmful pollution of a crowded modern city choked by automobile emissions. Acid rain gradually chips away the sculptures on the façades of the world's great cathedrals. Vandalism and even unmonitored tourism can also have a detrimental effect. The seemingly indestructible marble of Washington's Lincoln Memorial has worn down with the weight of the thousands of footsteps that cross its threshold, and graffiti scars its side.

It is obvious that the world's treasures must be saved. But preservationists have different philosophies about what should be done. Should ancient monuments that were meant to be

RIGHT: The Gothic-style construction of the monument to novelist and poet Sir Walter Scott in Edinburgh, Scotland, soars overhead, almost dwarfing the statue resting beneath.

outdoor public structures be moved to a sterile, climate-controlled museum? Should throngs of visitors be barred from experiencing some of the world's greatest monuments? Will the Vietnam War Memorial or the Grande Arche de la Défense survive as long as the pyramids of Giza?

UNESCO, the international organization that manages the World Monuments Fund, maintains an updated list of monuments that are in dire need of repair, preservation, and even more dramatic rescues. National and local governments as well as private organizations fund preservation and restoration projects. But it is up to individuals to be aware of the importance of the world's monuments and to ensure the endurance of today's monuments into the future. Only one of the Seven Wonders of the Ancient World survived five thousand years into the twentieth century. Which of today's monuments will survive into the next millennium?

ABOVE: In the Valley of the Kings in Giza, Egypt, the forty-five-hundred-year-old majestic pyramids form tombs for the ancient Egyptian pharaohs Mycerinus, Chephren, and Cheops. In addition to the remains of these rulers, the tombs originally contained everyday items the ancient Egyptians believed the soul would need in the afterlife.

INDEX